Changing Horizons

– MK GODBOLE –

An environmentally friendly book printed and bound in England by
www.printondemand-worldwide.com

This book is made entirely of chain-of-custody materials

www.fast-print.net/store.php

Changing Horizons

ISBN 978-178035-284-8

First published 2012 by
FASTPRINT PUBLISHING
Peterborough, England.

Contents

Foreword

Sometimes the poems scan like riddles, chopping and changing, repeating, leading you up a garden path then leaving you stranded, always best read aloud. Sometimes they scan like stepping stones across a cold mountain stream. Step carefully because they are wobbly, slippery and deceiving, like the path to truth in the first poem where, in conclusion, he states 'the truth is that I forgot I am a lover of the truth' – a beautiful amnesia that reminded me of something an elderly gentleman told me on a crowded bus in a jam waiting to go to Kalighat in Calcutta more than thirty years ago. I was stating the cause for atheism. He said 'But before there was God there was Kali'. Indeed, truth is always somewhere beyond.

I loved the humour of Sachinji's denial in 'The Justice of the Unjust' and the questioning sadness of finding a dead sparrow on the doorstep of an alien instead of a British thug. Emotionally rich, the riddles continue through fatigue of the relentless march of time in 'The Hand That

Feeds' until 'finally he has his say to turn me servile , to give in and obey.' There are only a few who escape this fact of life; we search and strive, we travel the seven seas and struggle and reach out, but in the end we 'give in and obey.' Then there is the yearning of the old to return to an imagined idyllic past, to Narayan's Malgudi. There were never merciless money-lenders in the Malgudi of the selective memory, there was plenty of food and the axle on the cart never broke.

In 'A Plea For Poetry' I could almost hear someone phoning Radio Four and complaining that we all want the easy way out, we don't want to be asked to think, we prefer Bollysong to Dhrupad, baseball to cricket. The whole world is becoming culturally lazy; we all seem to want everything simplified and quick to access – 'Confront they a poem they take to their heels.'

The seventh poem jolted me. After all it is titled 'Unexpected.' When travelling on the subcontinent with my wife we have always made friends, been invited to stay with people we have never even met and been fed and made welcome as if we were taking refuge from some terrible storm. I thought what friends have I got back home whose name and address I could give to these people if they were travelling in the UK and I was not there. There were none. I felt shame, my culture diminished. 'A waste of coins for the West' and a jolting affirmation of the lack of connection between people that prevents the culture that I emerged from finding it a 'joy to meet strangers.'

The jaunty questions in 'Whose Fault' presented an easier ride because the drinker blames everything but himself.

He would even blame the glass rather than himself. From pitying the half-lived life of the dyspeptic we are transported from the earthy to the ethereal where the 'expanse of the globe overhead, the clear blue dome' is 'all embracing.' Then back to earth with 'My Age, I Said' and the assured calm that age and wisdom bring, an intuition where you can see how things are going to end up but you cannot change the course. The poem 'Continued' has a horrible amount of blank space on the page, something familiar to most parents trying to encourage their children to finish their homework. From the idol youth to the reflective elderly person and a sturdy elm tree whose life is but a blink in the eye of Gods, even the sun cannot last. The reflective elderly person in 'Unnoticed' 'puts his feet up and bows his head down' and admits to having a 'high voltage' as opposed to the 'watch and wait of past medical men' but the poems turn from regret with a light humour because 'To say on its behalf I have a sound counsel in my other half.' Two opposites make a greater whole.

The emotional range of the poems thus far has for the most part included a fragility, a weariness, an aged wisdom, a sadness and self-reflection but 'Left Out' is an exaltation in the old Publish and Be Damned loud voice, telling us to stand up and be counted, or be left out – 'Publish and be Famed'.

They work best when read out loud. 'Greeting' bounces along , a merry tease with a satisfied conclusion and 'Mahesh Yogy's Yoga' scans playfully to echo sentiment – how to maintain a calm interior when the outside world dissolves into chaos.

'Put Your House In Order' is not so bouncy and playful. Indeed, it is 'a daylight thuggery, the British Way'. Compassion shines through the 19th poem, 'Rubbing Shoulders' and makes me think about genetics, environment, caste and class, the way the cards are dealt, luck and bad luck, karma. Compassion opens the mind and makes us see potential in people who have never had opportunity, gifts unnoticed and unseeable through a curtain of prejudice – 'Mixing with the infra digs is to dig into a mine of talent, ambition and mirth.'

The NHS is a lament for a great institution suffering under funding cuts and unable to perform at its best across the breadth of its customer base so that it leaves itself open to string-pulling, 'The civilised corruption.'

The last poem in the book is, compared to all the others, an epic. It is a huge task to undertake – to resolve the feelings the author had as a child with the feelings of the elderly statesman looking at his homeland from a great distance, looking at this terrible slice of history when one country imposes its will on another, creates an illusion of civilisation and elegance to cover up the wicked deed, and indulges in an arrogance and lack of self introspection that was common to the next empire and will probably be common to the next one again. 'Was it not all a sham? Was it not all a whitewash?' Of course it was but history repeats itself. The poem reminds me of a time when I was walking through the desolate streets of Stoke-on-Trent with a Tamil doctor friend on the way back to his house and I asked him, 'Don't you find it incredible that this lot could ever have run an empire when they can hardly run their own country?' He laughed at me and said,

'These days they can hardly run a bath.' Although the poem acknowledges that there was some good, some rays of light, the feeling I got from reading it aloud was that the whole thing was a bit of a bad dream, a sham, an illusion, a massive injustice and an embarrassing presumption of worth. But there's something missing – this is caste. It was an assumption of the high caste boys at public schools that they would inherit the earth. The working class was there to look after their horses and to do the dirty work. The ancient civilisation of India was unknown, purposely unknown, it was there to be plundered it was a place you could get a good job when you could find nothing like that at home. How the wheel of fate goes round and round, the tables are turned, Jaguar and Landrover are Tata now and Nataraj dances on and on and on.

The horizons are indeed changing. They have always changed and always will. It is difficult to maintain one's balance and more difficult still as we get older. These poems are slippery stepping stones, riddles, observations from a different angle, proclamations and questions. Read them aloud and I am sure you will enjoy as much as I have. We all need to 'change horizons' from time to time.

David Thomas

Preface

I am extremely indebted to Mr. David Thomas of Wales for finding time to write a Foreword to this book.

As a freelance journalist he wrote for The Times, The Financial Times and The Guardian, to name but a few.

Our family friend Girish Janai has played just as important a role in the publication of this book. He has literally guided my hand on to the computer keys, thereby unlocking the miraculous technology of this century.

Of Truth

Is it one side of a coin
Or third of a prism fine?
Is it untruth or half truth?

For Hindus there are three truths
One lasting.
Day follows night
Needs no testing

Truth of those times
Needs digging out like the mines.
Seem they with no bottom lines.

Truth of the present
Take it or resent
But take it not on it's face value.
That to be trusted
Is the funds, of rulers rusted.

Truth. Did you hear it
From one near,
Or reached it ear to ear?

Truth. “Read it I in black and white”
“I heard it on B.B.C.
Always right, always right.”
Like the old fable
Of elephant and blind men.
He who held the tail
Inferred the beast
Was brush like, wavy
Another held the tusks
Affirmed, it was biting, unsavoury.

The Shastras preach
Say out the truth
If it charms.
Say no more
If it harms.

Is it the truth,
The whole truth
And nothing but...
Asks the court
With a hand, on the Bible
Is it a foible
A trap, for the gullible?
Is there a lie- detector in it?

The truth is that
I forgot I am a lover of truth.

The Justice Of The Unjust

On a day with thoughts out of gripe
I threatened the Prime Minister with a hunger strike.

For what? he said
For the corruption
In his own coin I repaid.
"Which one?"
"The recent one,
Is it all cleared now, I queried"
Well, the press is busy with
Norway, The Mid East and India
And all that goes therewith.

And if corruption be still here
It is a Govt. and not a
National issue. He made it clear.
Wait you now, a six month referral
To a Specialist
Or soon such madness you quit.

But I tell you what.
A good cause you will find in the Umpire
They could not catch him nor stump or
Bowl him out. As Sachin neared his
Long, long track. A century of centuries.

The British raised false alarms. Out, Out,
Their cries shook the ground
And the viewers too. Twice the Umpire denied. But
The third shout was louder still.
Loud enough to twist his arm.
To raise the finger.

The command of Saint Andrew now rang
Back in his ear. Andrew Strauss
The Captain had said, "We shall never ever
Allow Sachin's century on our Lawful Land"

It dazed Sachin. Stood he confused,
Then walked back to a sympathetic applause.

The world's most revered batsman
Never ever can British justice
Tarnish his image. A century he lost
Yet in stature he gained.

By now he was used to the tradesman's justice
And of their ancestral hoodlums, the Australians.

The P.M. said, although we claim
We invented the game.
It were the Belgians who did.

We send the offenders to their own country to be tried.
So we now pack you to India.
So Bye- Bye.

A Sparrow On My Doorstep

On a hot clear day
A sparrow laid it's corpse, in my way
Laid it sideways.
But what was that? Did I see a stir of it's wing?
Or was it the wind of spring?

Though a doctor. It stirred me not to my stethoe
A non lover of non humans I leant on thought
Of insects it had brought.
The chestpiece I use to ascertain life
I would use instant asepsis rife.

Not instructed in Conan Doyle, my detective ability
Didn't surpass doctor Watson's quality.
Homicide or suicide?
Not the former. I inferred. No cat bite or blood congealed
Well. Why did it choose my house. Sneaked like a mouse
An alien like me? why not a British thug?

I think I have already said. I'm not an animal lover.
Yet the last rites are not yet over
A funeral as an option, would misfire.
The dry grass would set the neighbour's house afire.

Chose I a spot in the backyard.
The back right corner of the yard
Dug it three feet down.
Laid the sparrow with a covering
Of soil, fish and bone, soil, fish and bone and again soil
fish and bone.
Then planted a perennial to yield flowers best.
And left the soul to rest.
A white placard I placed.
May you serve in death.

The Hand That Feeds

Kingdoms and empires rise and fall.
The British Raj too, went with yell.
But now beware. The Robotic Raj
Is here to stay and overstay.
So they say.

This is how I do it, you say
Learns he, day after day.
Till finally he has his say
To turn me servile. To give in and obey.

Lock would it me in the closet
While it proof reads
My poems
Do we know

What path would they choose
Most sane and sound
Or to blast bombs bound.

It Harks Back

The faster the train moves
The speedier the globe spins back
In India, it brings aback
The past days' memory
In a village.
The fancied spot
Of carefree life in a cottage
Serene, clean, and basking in the sun.

The bane of mankind, it is.
The bane of mankind, it is
To look back at the golden past
It is man's downward pull
Of gravity. Greater than the will.

Divorce they the reality
The frailty and cruelty
The farmer encounters.
The landlord paying wages poor

The money lender taking more
Than his fair share
Several thumb impressions
Spins the rustic out of his wits

Untimely rain, and untimely shine
Leaves him little to dine.

No breakdown service for the yoke
None for the man, or the beast
The children leave for the town
And he lays his soul down.

A Plea For Poetry

Strange it is to see
Those poetry estrange
Believe it not as you may.
There are men
Men of learning
Mannered speech of noble thoughts
And nobler deeds. Who shy away from poetry.

Read and read as they do
As a need or leisure
But not them a poem for pleasure.

Can't grasp it, they say
Though a film song they sing or hum
Much too humdrum
Or when hear they on reels.
Confront they a poem
They take to their heels.

Unexpected

Sheltered in a warm spot
Screened off we sat
In a restaurant.

Through my left eye
Spied I
A mid aged figure
Clad in a sari, scarlet red
To go with an eye catching
Mark on her forehead, fair.
Such matching colours
Seen I have. But rare.

A beaded necklace. With a locket dear.
Spoke it of her faith.
So too a wedding symbol.
Tendered with dignity and care.
My heart leaped within. And stirred me from my seat.
I got off to greet her

Led me she to a table for four.
The couple, and a newly wed son.

They pressed me their hospitality
To partake.
The fabled generosity of the East
A waste of coins for the West.
A treat to an acquaintance? Never.

She went to fetch my family.
She had met not ever.
We acquired the contact numbers.
Chatted over and over.

It's a joy to meet strangers
Of your land.
Some ask me, why do I bother.
"At times I get a jolt, lasting friends at other."

Whose Fault?

The cosy bed.
Beckons me back.
Yet against its will,
I rise.
Reflect and Realise.

How hard it be. To those who end
The day, with a burrah peg
Or a bottle full.

Spend half a day in light. Half in dark .
A chit chat, slip slap and a noticeable nap.
Do precious little to mark.
For self. Or else.

Whom do they blame? As they pass?
Their friends, themselves,
Or the glass?

As I Lie Down

As I lie. Backside down
In my glass house,
Awed I am by the expanse
Of the globe overhead.
The clear blue dome. All embracing.

The un-bathed clouds.
The sun, washing them white
Down to the chest.
A hand clean car wash.

The metallic bonnet spotless
Yet the rest dusty grey
As the rays sprinkle
Their spray.
More clouds, wait their turn
As the washer man moves from one to one.

In the eve I view clouds.
Alien. Non whites. Non blacks.
With a golden lining.
Of the golden sun.
Journeying past the hill.

"My Age , I Said"

In the sixties
We were in fifties
I and my wife.

A close friend we had.
Indian. Eight years young.
The couple was affable.
Welcome guests.
And open armed hosts.
Their two children
Straight and docile,
Gentle and facile.

One day they announced
A LONG holiday.
With another couple
And two kids.
Strangers to us
Yet close to them.

Returned all in a WEEK.
"Did it end in a fight?"
I asked.
With a puzzled look
She asked, "Who told you?"

My age, I said.

Continued.

He stood before the desk
For Home Work not done.

He stood before her
For Home Work half done.

The Elm Tree

The sturdy tree
Sways its arms in joy
As the wind whistles
Or stands it to attention
As the elements dictate.

The Elm tree
Bathed in the sun
Grave and erect
Sings no song in a mode
As I watch it from my abode.

Overhead moving clouds
Dark and dismal
Bring they a merry breeze
With a white dove or two.

The Elm waves a hand
Like the Queen mother

To passers by.

Watch I its garb of gold and green, Regal.
A spectacle , not long to last.
Then the final Fall.

The Elm tree. Parks a pigeon rare, on it's
shoulder bare. Two bikes with yellow stripes
black seats and shiny wheels, lean on its trunk.

By it the Silver beach demure, Stands censured
Female rights ignored. Dressed it is in silky white
Three black buttons out-standing. Each a mark of a fallen
branch.

Unnoticed

Now is the age, now is the time,
Put your feet up bow your head down.

Points fore 'The Finger Reflex'
To one Mr. X.
I grew up with it .Points it back to me
When I gobble, in greed
Or swallow in I shame
When it comes to blame.

The more it points in
The more I meditate
Should I have kept shut
When I argued with that nut?
No reason could I see
To rethink .To hesitate.

Now in my state
I know I lack the gift

Of cool reflection
But down the war path
Rush I.

I go through bouts of seeming emotion
Tears well up to my eyes
The voice sinks
As a thing drops or dies.

I want in political acumen
No watch and wait of past Medical men
Reactive and inflammable am I
Carry on me a voltage high.

To say on it's behalf
I have a sound counsel
In my other half.

Left Out

The line is thin, barely seen
Fact and fiction between
As you write on kith and kin.

Clearly you live in wrong times
If time was ever right.
To flow with the flow.
No trumpet to blow
Your spouse alone is left to know
Your expertise. In pleural.
On A.I.R. a noted classical singer
And Sitarist. Now held back by age
And unyielding knees.

A multinational chef you are
Still left for the masses to test and taste
Your improvised recipes.
In the book waiting to print.
Hurry up and be counted.

By God. There is no fiction in
What I say. Though late, I urge
You to write in earnest. Though
Late I need to blow the trumpet

May be you had one string too many to
Your bow.

I adore you for your fortitude.
'Sangeet Visharad' sings for
your musical altitude.
Here I stand corrected
Times indeed have changed
PUBLISH AND BE FAMED.

Greetings

The British downed by the weather
Wish you Good Morn /Noon /or eve.
The Yankees bent to differ
Brief it all in Good Day

We confront a man with regards,
Namaste or Salaam we say
Rain, shine or snow
Wherever we go
We give and take regards

Ladies in the West
Are objects of sex
Hullo Madam or Miss

The Hindoos know
How to address a female,
They don't know.
Call they Sister or Mum.....

For us respect
Is the substance and sum.

Mahesh Yogy's ! Yoga

Ageing men grumble
Help their physique to crumble
Sow they the seed
Of grumbleweed.

Needs it weeding out.
For a greener lawn
On their side of the fence.

They look out. The sky lies dark.
Within, a power cut.
Out there a hailstorm,
Within them a thunderstorm.

Find they the kitchen too small
To wobble between table and worktop
With bellies puffed with food and wine.

The sitting room noisy with the Box.

The dining, a grandchild's playground
And waffle.

Two bedrooms, fighting sons and wives
His own shakes with discord. A cacophony.

Time is ripe to learn, the oddities of beings.
Yoga needs he and the rest.
To keep poise and peace.
A voice of his would add no melody but
Discord. Of views.

Put Your House In Order

The England of one time glory
And one time fame
Now dragged down to be sorry
For good. Dejected and downcast.

The phrased Englishman's word
Obsolete in the land.

Now the white man, seeks a way
To loot and dupe
The brown, black and white.
For one and all a sad sight.

A bank and company
Well in company
Lets down the client
Through a fake promise.

Find they ways to payments
Due, to prolong undue
And pray for the old or infirm's demise!

Take you a leaf, from
The men of The Raj
Yet lack you the knack
Of British craft
To hide the sins under a draft.
Lo, now its all in open
A daylight thuggery
The British way.

Rubbing Shoulders

The Top Brass is a clan on it's own.
To rub shoulders with, the middle class
Aspires. The poor serves them both.
And perspires.

Oh. What a treat it is to share a meal
With such a family .
A worthy gardener, a cleaner, window
Cleaner or a handyman.

Nice to know what quirk of fate turned
Them to their calling and their state.
Graduates are some. The onus of family
Left them no dallying.

Mixing with the infra digs
Is to dig into a mine of
Talent, ambition and mirth.

Cricket players, budding poets, writers
Guitarists or singers. Such hobbies they
Do pursue. Which you and I wont view.

All said. Why are they infra digs to us or above?
Is it not fate to grant us a “silver spoon
And them a wooden ladle”?

The N.H.S

Learnt I a lot from N.H.S.
In Health Care an ace
Or so we thought at birth
Now ailing, ageing under Govt's mirth.
Ripening now to die from dearth
And misuse of public funds,
Millions of pounds down the
Miracle drain. It never blocks.

Learned I a lot from N.H.S.
As a doctor
And now at the receiving end,
With my joints refusing to bend,
Bellows reluctant to breathe.

The dying heart seeks a bypass
The ageing red tape
Replete with drafts
In no rush to pass to the Master

Of the crafts.
I for one shunting from pillar to post.

The bypass twice delayed
Helpless. At home I laid.
Eighty miles away through a doctor I knew,
Pulled I the strings.
The "Old Boy" network
To make things work,
The civilised way.
The civilised corruption!

In India too its not new.
Know one
OR
Pay one.

Learnt I a lot from N.H.S.
Germs gened and bright,
Keep a count of day and night
Attack they at end of a week,
Then they best play an evil trick.

G.P.s rest like Gods.
A doctor calls
In Six hours or beyond. At an hour odd

Writes he a thing or two.
When muddled
"Ring your G.P.
too, on Monday."

Emergency as yet is
Best dealt by 999
A trained Ambulance team
Fully equipped
Leave they nothing to “Ifs or buts.”

Learnt I a lot from N.H. S.
The N.H.S.
Lived it on a monthly cut
From our salary
Covered it all our health needs yearly.

Now its hard, on the hard ups.
Choose do they between some seven pounds per
Rx. or their daily grub.

The British And A Native Boy

For once I shall not dip my pen, in the gall of the Raj.
For once I shall not, let my native pride to override
My hatred of the British Raj.
For once shall I give the devil's due
And not paint him black undue.
Unlike the film Gandhi.

The British were a clever race, under the queen.
Brought they the three piece suit, a tie and a tea-cosy
In the tropical heat. With rituals like these, they
Could not be choosey.

Men so few. Ruled the land so new.
Made they their goal to renew.
By choice of the highest wisdom,
In all castes and creeds
Yet the low class men that were to land
A job could not they suit in their motherland.

The Whites. A mere handful I knew.
When as a child I grew.
Others I merely watched
Curiously, as the parade of trumpets passed.
On the streets.

Senior ranks were for Whites.
Junior for non whites.
Save my dad's.
Whites were bad (I suppose).
Lacked they the skill Surgical
And acumen Medical.
Thus we landed in an English thatched house.
Shared it overhead with a futile race
Between reptiles and a mouse.

Bestowed on my dad was a R.B.
A gold watch, he never used
And an engraved grain of rice.
The tiny grain stood for every
Grain of his being.

The British I knew as a child were few.
Cultured were they.
Kept vanity at bay.

Facing us in his humble abode lived Mr. Syke
Owned he a motor-bike. As a Police chief he
Raced to catch an absconding absconder.
I watched him keenly, as a bystander
And wondered the game he would play
His pistol, he was prone to display.

Mrs. Syke kept up her Sunday evening visits.
When children were to be seen and not heard
I was too keen to catch each word. To add to
Mine. My job was to get three cane chairs
Lined by tyres, all-round.
For her and my parents to chat on the ground.
She sat dutifully an hour and left to cook her
Man a Sunday dinner.

I would linger, spin the top
Or saunter. I had my ears around me.
While they talked over nuts and tea.
At Xmas a cake with icing she would send
My mum our chosen sweets exchanged.

On the outskirts lay
A solitary circuitous way
Of a mile. I often ran to catch up with my dad.
I would often pant. All said it was not too bad.
The D.C. coming the other way would raise his
Hat with a smile. My father bareheaded nodded awhile,

Rarely the D.C. was seen with his wife. They. The mem-
sahibs
How tall were they all, thought I.
Did the men have no say? On their diminished heads??
Their dimmed image .Dimmed by those stiletto heels, I
Was unaware of.

Seldom we dropped in at the D.C.'s house. Had tea and
biscuits
On the house .Well beyond me was his talk.

I used to leave and walk.
What a riot of colours did his garden display!
Dahlias, Tulips, Lillies, Roses, Marigold and Bougainvillaea.
Mingled here East and West
And they blossomed best!

At my Dada's wedding were 400 men.
A bit beyond my ken.
Amongst dignitaries, the D.C. inclusive.
His table for one
Stood on the veranda.

On a well broomed ground laid long strips of rolled out fabric
We sat on them like yogis.
Wherever a place we found
Save the first three ranks.
Rangoli made a dainty surround
To silver thalis, katoris and glass.
The rest were content with banana leaves
And brass dinner set.

A fragrant joss stick
Burnt on potato slice
Beside each seat you could pick.
An Indian dinner, lasts and lasts with liberal servings.
The sweets don't come last but times uncounted.

Amazed were we
The D.C. to see
Join our ranks.

Cross legged sat he
Shoeless.
A down to earth man!

Beside Mr. Syke's was the officers' club
Went I with my dad
Tennis he played
In the library I stayed
Struck with Dickens' and others' wisdom.

Post tennis was a toast to The Queen.
My father. A glass of water he raised.

No eyebrows it raised
A due regard they paid.

But now with a hindsight,
I am foxed.

Were the British so good
As the native boy found?
Did not the film Gandhi portray
Them true and sound?

Unwittingly before my time violence was rife.
Shooting and crucifixion had shaken The Raj
The party was over, Stopped the rulers to be braver.

All I saw. All I heard. All I perceived.
Was it not all a sham?
Was it not all a whitewash?
All. All. All.

Glossary

1. Hindu- A follower of Hinduism-polytheistic religion of India.
2. B.B.C.- British Broadcasting Corporation.
3. Shastras- Sacred Hindu writings (In Sanskrit).
4. Bible- Scriptures of the Old and New Testament.
5. Burrah Peg- Large peg of wine.
6. He stood before her- As an adult he stood before his wife.
7. A.I.R.- All India Radio.
8. Sitarist- One who has attained professional skill in Sitar (Indian string instrument).
9. Sangeet Visharad- Graduate in North Indian Classical Music as against the South Indian Karnatic Music.

10. Yoga- Hindu system of philosophic meditation, and asceticism designed to effect reunion of the devotees' soul with the universal spirit.

11. To loot- Goods taken from enemy, plunder.

12. Thuggery- Cut throat practitioner, ruffian.

13. Top Brass- Those who are richest and/or highest in position.

14. Infra digs- Beneath one's dignity, unbecoming.

15. N.H.S.- National Health Service.

16. G.P.- General Practitioner (in Medicine)

17. 999**-** No. to dial in an emergency for Police, Health or Fire**.**

18. Rx- Prescription.

19. R.B.- Rao Bahadur- A title given to Indians by the British (equivalent to O.B.E.) for good service to them.

20. D.C.- District Commissioner during British Raj.

21. Dada- In India the eldest brother is addressed as Dada.

22. Veranda- Open portico or gallery along side of the house with roof supported on pillars.

23. Yogi- Devotee of Yoga.

24. Rangoli- Decorative drawings made by coloured powder of stones in the foreground during festivity in India.

25. Silver thalis, katoris- In India during festivity silver plates and bowls are used to serve food.

26. Joss sticks- Fragrant sticks which are burnt during worship or festivity.

27. Crucifixion- A movement called Patri Sarkar started by Nana Patil in Maharashtra.

ND - #0270 - 080726 - C0 - 197/132/5 - PB - 9781780352848 - Gloss Lamination